ALOHA!

For all of us who cherish the
wild, fresh beauty of
the Hawaiian forests and the
great variety of plants that
grow in the uplands of our
majestic mountains, we
welcome you to share
in the joy of discovery.

NAHELE O HAWAI'I

NO KA 'OI

Red Ginger
'awapuhi-'ula'ula
Alpinia purpurata

Kukui trees (Aleurites moluccana)

THE ILLUSTRATED PLANTS

This guide presents many of the common native and alien plants found in the forests and other inland areas of Hawai'i. Additional plants are included as examples of unique, interesting, rare, or endangered native species. The plants have been arranged according to their general distribution along a gradient of elevation and rainfall. Those occurring in the drier lowlands and lower mountain slopes come first. These are followed by plants of the moderately moist regions. Finally, species found in wet forest areas and drier high elevation places are depicted and described.

INDEX TO PLANTS - *Hawaiian or English names, and page numbers*

SYMBOL LEGEND

(I) Indigenous native plant - arrived in Hawai'i without human help, but also native elsewhere;

(E) Endemic native plant - evolved from indigenous Hawaiian species, only found in Hawai'i;

(P) Polynesian introduction - brought to Hawai'i by people during the prehistoric period (before 1778);

(R) Recent alien introduction - brought to Hawai'i by people after 1778.

Swamp mahogany (Eucalyptus robusta)

'Ilima (I)
Sida fallax
Family: Malvaceae

Description

This small shrub species (1-5 ft. tall) is hardy and variable. It grows prostate (*'ilima papa*) on the ground, often near the seashore, and upright (*'ilima kū kula*) in arid plains and lower dry forest. It has 1/2 to 1 inch wide, yellow-orange flowers and ovate, light green, serrated leaves, with or without dense, tiny soft hairs.

Distribution

'Ilima is a native plant on many Pacific islands, especially in more arid locations. For example, it is common on Wake Island, which the people of the Marshall Islands refer to as Enen Kio ("island of *'ilima*"). In Hawai'i, this indigenous plant occurs in open, dry areas from sea level to about 6,000 ft.

Uses

The lovely flowers of *'ilima* were strung into royal *lei* for chiefly ornament. They are still used to make highly-valued garlands, although it takes about 500 flowers to make one *lei*, and they wilt by the second day. As a medicinal source, the flowers of *'ilima* were sometimes used to cure general debility, womb disorders, and asthma. Juice squeezed out the flowers is used as a gentle baby laxative called *kanakamaika'i*. *'Ilima* is the flower of O'ahu Island.

'A 'ali'i (I)

Dodonaea viscosa
Family: Sapindaceae

Description

As one of its Hawaiian names (*'a 'ali'i kūmakani*) suggests, this is a royal plant that stands up against the wind. It is variable in form reaching heights of 6-25 feet with leaves 1-4 inches long. It is the only native, deep tap-rooted plant in Hawai'i. Bright red, rose or yellowish, capsular, fruit clusters give this woody dry forest shrub an ornamental aspect.

Distribution

'A 'ali'i is a wide ranging indigenous species in many tropical areas including Hawai'i, where it is found in a variety of different environments, from near sea level to about 7,000 ft. elevation, on all main islands except Kaho'olawe.

Uses

'A 'ali'i was a sacred plant of the hula goddesses *Laka* and *Kapo*. The beautiful, light red fruits were strung into head *lei* woven with ferns. The woody parts of *'a 'ali'i* are very hard and durable. Larger branches were used for building timbers and making weapons. If a red tapa (*kapa*) cloth dye was needed, the Hawaiians could collect the bright red *'a 'ali'i* capsules and boil them in water held in calabashes and heated by hot stones until a red stained liquid was produced. Also used medicinally, *'a 'ali'i* leaves were crushed and applied to rashes and itches as an infusion with other plant materials.

Koa haole (R)
Leucaena leucocephala
Family: Fabaceae

Description

Koa haole is a shrub or small tree (also known as *ēkoa* or *lilikoa*), up to 30 ft. tall or more. It bears globular white flower heads roughly one inch in diameter, has compound leaves with many leaflets, and produces bunches of long, thin pods that enclose numerous brown seeds.

Distribution

Koa haole, a member of the pea or bean family, is native to tropical America, but has been spread by humans to several other tropical areas of the world. It was introduced into the Hawaiian lowlands and dry forests early in the 19th century and is a prime example of an alien species which has successfully invaded extensive areas in the Hawaiian Islands.

Uses

In Hawai'i, *koa haole* has served as a cattle feed and the seeds are strung into garlands (*lei*). In addition, botanists have noted that stands of *koa haole* offer shade for natural regeneration of native species, and as a legume, it acts as a host for nitrogen fixing bacteria that attach themselves to the roots. Thus it is known as a nurse crop. However, it has become an aggressive pest and now dominates many lowland areas of Hawai'i.

Lantana, *Lakana* (R)

Lantana camara
Family: Verbenaceae

Description

This thorny shrub usually reaches heights of 3 to 6 feet but can grow up to more than 15 feet tall. Clustered into compact heads, the small tubular flowers vary in color from yellow, orange, white, and pink to red. Hikers will recognize the attractive flowers and the pungent smell of this plant, but will find it very troublesome to move through because of its dense and prickly growth.

Distribution

A native of tropical America, lantana grows over exposed areas in the lower mountain forests up to about 3,000 ft., in moist as well as dry habitats. It was introduced into Hawai'i as an ornamental plant in 1858. Since then, lantana has become a severe pest here, and is now naturalized on all main islands and Midway Atoll. Spread by berry-feeding birds and other dispersal agents, lantana is now one of the most common weedy plants in the tropics.

Guava, *Kuawa* (R)
Psidium guajava
Family: Myrtaceae

Description

The guava plant is an alien shrub or small tree up to about 30 ft. tall, with spreading branches. It produces leaves 3 to 6 inches long and flowers with 1/2 to 1 inch long white petals and numerous stamens. The fruit is 1-4 inches long with an irregular yellowish surface, edible pink flesh, and many tough seeds.

Distribution

A very common plant in many of the wet, lower forests, this tropical American species has been in Hawai'i since the early 1800's. In some moderately moist areas where cattle, horses, pigs, and birds feed, fast-growing guava has become a serious weed that has crowded out native vegetation. However, it is not as common as its close relative, the strawberry guava, which was also introduced to Hawai'i in the 19th century.

Uses

Guava leaf buds are sometimes used to make a medicinal tea, and the nutritious, valuable fruit is used to make jellies, jams, and juice with a high content of vitamin C.

Strawberry Guava (R)
Waiawī ʻulaʻula

Psidium cattleianum
Family: Myrtaceae

Description

The strawberry guava is a small tree, up to about 20 ft. tall. It has smooth bark, shiny, dark green leaves, white flowers with numerous stamens, and oval fruits (1/2 to 1 inch in diameter) that turn dark red or yellowish when they ripen.

Distribution

Introduced from tropical America, strawberry guava grows in thick clumps on all the major islands in the moderately wet forests. Three forms are naturalized in Hawaiʻi, one red-fruited (*waiawī ʻulaʻula*) and 2 yellow-fruited (*waiawī*, upper right photo).

Uses

Although strawberry guava fruits are quite tasty when ripe, this plant is a troublesome pest. It has sturdy branches, produces abundant fruit, forms dense stands, crowds out other plants, and lacks its natural enemies in our isolated island environments. Alien birds, wild pigs, and humans consume the fruit and disperse the seed of this plant, and thus have greatly enlarged the range of distribution of strawberry guava in Hawaiʻi. This species is a serious threat to some of the unique native Hawaiian plant species.

Ironwood, *Paina* (R)
Casuarina spp.
Family: Casuarinaceae

Description

The common, but alien, ironwood (*Casuarina equisetifolia*, sometimes known as "beefwood" or "she oak") is a fast growing tree, reaching heights of more than 60 ft. within 10 years. The bark is light to dark gray. The trunk wood is dark red and very tough. Ironwood does not have true leaves. Its "needles" are actually thread-shaped, jointed, greenish branchlets. Note the tiny, brownish, teeth-like organs at each branchlet joint. These are degenerate leaves. During May and June, male and female flowers are borne separately. The small male flowers form brownish cylinder-like tips at the ends of some branchlets. The small female flowers form red clusters at the base of the branchlets. The fruits are cone-like in shape, about 1/2 inch in length, and turn brown as they ripen.

Distribution

Native to Northern Australia, ironwood is cultivated and naturalized in many tropical and subtropical regions. It is found in many areas throughout the drier environments of Hawai'i from sea level up to above 3,000 ft. Another common, ironwood tree now naturalized in the Hawaiian Islands is *Casuarina glauca*.

Uses

In many areas of Hawai'i, alien ironwood has been planted as a rapid growing tree for watershed protection. Although it is used as an effective windbreak and a soil or sand binder, it often grows into a thick stand that virtually chokes out the growth of almost all other plants. Its tough roots can also break up pavement. In other islands of the Pacific region, where it was probably introduced in prehistoric times, ironwood is a source of medicine because of the high tannin concentration in its astringent bark; and its dense, hard wood has been used to make war clubs, spears, tapa beaters, and other artifacts.

The male flowers of the ironwood tree

The common Polynesian name of ironwood is *toa*. In Hawaiian, this word (*koa*) refers to bravery, warrior, or the native *Acacia koa* tree. The Hawaiian word for ironwood, *paina*, comes from the English word for pine; but *Casuarina* is not in the same family as any pine (*Pinus*) or other true cone-bearing plant. Pine and ironwood trees were only introduced to Hawai'i after 1778.

The fruit of the ironwood tree

Christmas Berry (R)
Brazilian Pepper, *Wilelaiki*

Schinus terebinthifolius
Family: Anacardiaceae

Description
This small tree or shrub can grow to heights over 20 feet. Its gnarled trunk supports branches which bear five to nine paired leaflets with an extra, larger one at the tip. Christmas berry is a dioecious species (i.e., male and female flowers are segregated on separate plants). Small yellow-greenish flower clusters usually develop in the summer on the female trees with abundant bright red clumps of berries following in the fall.

Distribution
A native of Brazil, Christmas berry grows like a weed in lowlands and arid upland forests of Hawai'i where it is now a serious pest, especially in waste areas and the dry mountain gulches. A prolific fruit producer, this plant is dispersed widely by birds and humans and is quite often found in association with other mountain weeds such as guava and lantana.

Uses
Although it is very aggressive, Christmas berry is grown as an ornamental. Its berry clusters are collected during the winter holiday season and woven into wreaths and garlands. Its Hawaiian name, *wilelaiki*, honors Willie Rice, who often wore a hat *lei* containing red Christmas berries while campaigning for political office.

Kiawe
Algaroba, Mesquite (R)
Prosopis pallida
Family: Fabaceae

Description

Kiawe is a shrub or tree, sometimes reaching heights over 50 feet. Variable in size and form, it often develops deep root systems which tap the ground water in dry areas. The trunk and branches often grow into twisted forms and the crown is large and wide-spreading. Its leaves are compound, comprising dozens of leaflets, and the tiny yellow flowers are borne on long, cylindrical spikes, usually during the spring. The fruit are stiff, yellowish and waxy. Hikers should watch out for the long sharp thorns. They may penetrate slippers and sandals, inflicting painful punctures.

Distribution

Kiawe is native to an area in South America. Some of its close relatives in the genus *Prosopis* (pea or bean family) are widespread in the New World. In Hawai'i, this alien woody plant is common along sandy shores, arid plains, and the drier mountain slopes of all the main Hawaiian Islands up to almost 2,000 ft. (see photograph below showing *kiawe* dominating a leeward alluvial plain and upland dry forest area of East Moloka'i).

Uses

First introduced in Hawai'i by Father Bachelot in 1828, *kiawe* has become a very common and useful tree. The wood makes an excellent fuel. The flowers provide nectar for bees which produce a tasty honey. The pods are nutritious fodder for hogs and cattle. And it is an important reforestation tree in the lower, dry forests. However, because they develop deep tap roots, these trees can lower the water table in some coastal areas.

Ōwī, Oī, Cayenne Vervain (R)
Stachytarpheta urticifolia
Family: Verbenaceae

Description and Distribution

This introduced perennial herb is occasionally woody near the base. It is a weedy spreading plant up to 4 ft. tall, with opposing leaves that are 2 to 4 inches long and have serrated margins. A thin floral spike produces the small, light to dark purplish or white flowers. The species shown here is usually found in shaded, moderately wet, disturbed areas from near sea level up to about 600 ft. elevation. Known as the cayenne vervain, this small alien plant is naturalized in many tropical and subtropical areas of the world. It is closely related to three other alien species in the genus *Stachytarpheta* that are also found growing wild in Hawai'i *(S. jamaicensis, S. mutabilis,* and *S. dichotoma). Stachytarpheta dichotoma* occurs up to 4,000 ft. above sea level in the Hawaiian Islands. Often bees and other insects can be seen visiting the flowers of these plants to feed on available nectar.

Fiddlewood (R)
Citharexylum caudatum
Family: Verbenaceae

Description and Distribution

Fiddlewood is a large shrub or small tree which produces stalks with clusters of small white flowers and orange fruit that turn purplish black when ripe. This tropical American plant was first introduced into Hawai'i in the upper region of Mānoa Valley in 1931. In a relatively short time this noxious species has spread widely (largely by birds) out of Mānoa Valley, and can now be found growing abundantly on the wet, leeward slopes of the Ko'olau Mts. If its short history on O'ahu is indicative, fiddlewood may well disperse much further and become another troublesome pest, threatening the unique (endemic) native plants of the Hawaiian Islands. Similar to *Lantana camara,* its relative in the verbena family, fiddlewood is a very aggressive, weedy species. Lantana and fiddlewood were both introduced into Hawai`i as ornamental plants, but like many other species, they have escaped cultivation and invaded forests or open areas in these islands.

Pūkiawe, ʻAʻaliʻi mahu, Maiele (I)
Kānehoa, Pukeawe, Pūpūkiawe, etc.

Styphelia tameiameiae
Family: Epacridaceae

Description

This native woody shrub or small tree-like plant, with short variable leaves, produces tiny rigid flowers and relatively dry, bright white, pink, or dark red fruits roughly 1/4 inch in diameter.

Distribution

Pūkiawe can be found growing in the drier forests as well as in the higher semi-arid subalpine scrub. Occasionally, *pūkiawe* inhabits exposed lava flows and open spots in the more humid environments. Above the tree line, *pūkiawe* extends farther up the mountain slopes than any other woody plant, in some places, higher than 10,000 ft. on Mauna Kea and Mauna Loa volcanoes. It also occurs in the Marquesas Islands.

Uses

Pūkiawe fruits are strung into *lei*. In old Hawaiʻi, the leaves were used in medicines, and outlaws were cremated with the wood. When a high-ranking chief (*aliʻi*) mixed with commoners (*makaʻāinana*), he would be marked with the soot of burnt *pūkiawe* wood, as a priest (*kahuna*) chanted a special prayer.

Pānini (**R**)
Prickly Pear

Opuntia ficus-indica
Family: Cactaceae

Description

Prickly pear cacti can reach heights of about 15 ft. with distinct trunks and jointed stems. They produce yellow or red flowers about 2-4 inches long and 1-3 inches wide. The fruit are greenish white to yellow, yellowish brown, or deep red, pear-shaped, and about 1.5 to 4 inches long. The cactus shown here is the most common of the three alien species of prickly pear cacti now naturalized in Hawai`i.

Distribution

Pānini (*Opuntia ficus-indica*) was introduced from Mexico about 1809 by Don Marin, a Spaniard and advisor to Kamehameha I. *Pānini,* with yellow flowers, occurs in dry disturbed lowlands and arid mountain slopes on Kaua`i, O`ahu, Maui, Kaho`olawe, and Hawai`i. By 1930, *pānini* had become a serious pest in many cattle pastures of Hawai`i. From 1949 to 1960, insects were introduced as a biological control. *Opuntia cochenillifera,* with red flowers, occurs in some low areas on Kaua`i and O`ahu.

Uses

As in Mexico, local people in Hawai`i have found the fruit of *pānini* to be a delicious treat, fresh or fermented and made into a drink. However, hikers should take care when handling the fruit. It produces numerous clumps of small yellowish-tan bristles that become embedded in the skin and can cause a rather painful irritation.

Pua kala, Kala, Naule, Pōkalakala **(E)**
Prickly Poppy
Argemone glauca
Family: Papaveraceae

Description

Pua kala, the native prickly poppy, is an erect, perennial herb that grows to heights of about 4 ft. The stems are somewhat woody, and many parts of the plant have a grayish appearance. The fruits and leaves are coarse and prickly. *Pua kala* produces flowers throughout much of the year. A center of yellowish-orange stamens and a red-tipped pistil add color to the white petals of the flower.

Distribution

Pua kala is an endemic species in Hawai'i. It usually grows in dry coastal forest, on rocky lower mountain slopes, and even in the subalpine forest on the main islands except Kaua'i. It also may be found in some cow pastures because it is one of very few native Hawaiian plants that produce thorns, barbs, spines or prickles. Most native Hawaiian plants probably lack natural defenses such as stiff prickles and thorns, or even poisons and strong odors because of the absence of large grazing or browing animals such as hoofed mammals which were introduced by humans, especially in historic times.

Uses

Like all members of the Poppy Family, this native Hawaiian prickly poppy produces active chemicals known as alkaloids. However, unlike its relative, the opium poppy (*Papaver somniferum*), the native Hawaiian poppy contains no morphine or codeine alkaloids. Traditionally, Hawaiians have used the seeds and yellowish stalk sap of *pua kala* for ulcers, toothache, and general nerve pain. The sap was also used to treat warts.

Ko'oko'olau, Kōko'olau, Ko'olau(E)
Bidens spp.
Family: Asteraceae

Description

There are many native Hawaiian species in the genus *Bidens*. All are closely related and belong to the daisy or sunflower family. They are perennial herbs, but lightly woody at the base, and produce flowering "heads" (capitula), often with five or more brilliant, yellowish petals (ray florets). Pairs of leaves are arranged opposite each other, vary in length, have serrated margins, and bear few or many hairs. The closed fruits (achenes) are dry and black or dark brown.

Distribution

There are 19 endemic *Bidens* species in Hawai'i. Most are known in Hawaiian as *ko'oko'olau*, or by other names listed above. *Bidens cosmoides*, only found on Kaua'i, has giant flowering heads (2 inches or more in diameter) and is known as *po'ola nui*. The native *Bidens* vary in their range of distribution from sea level to about 8,000 ft, and are found among the arid lava flows or dry forests as well as in the moist forest, especially in exposed habitats. *Bidens pilosa* ("beggar tick" or "Spanish needle"), known in Hawaiian as *kī* or *kī nehe*, is an alien weed from tropical America with two or three-pronged, straight-shaped fruit that easily become attached to people or animals; it is common in disturbed places, especially in or near urban areas. All of the native *Bidens* species apparently evolved from a single ancestor.

Uses

The leaves of native *ko'oko'olau* have long been used to make a common invigorating tea for those suffering from overexertion and stress. Leaves steeped in hot water and squeezed dry were mixed with warm sweet potatoes and coconut cooked with coconut milk and given to fatigued patients before some treatments. The flowers were used in medicinal recipes for general sickness and to stimulate an appetite. Parts of the native *Bidens* spp. were used in douches to aid women who had several miscarriages, and *ko'oko'olau* leaves were also among the green plant materials added to the diets of expectant mothers. Today, the alien *Bidens pilosa* is also used in local medicinal remedies. All native *Bidens* contain phototoxic polyacetylenes in their roots, as well as in the leaves of many species.

Wiliwili (E)

Erythrina sandwicensis
Family: Fabaceae

Description

Wiliwili trees range in height from about 15 to 30 ft. The trunks are often short, thick, twisted, and produce some thorns. Their branches bear ovate leaflets 2-3 inches wide. The leaflets drop off in the summer to avoid desiccation. Flowers are bright red, white, yellowish, or orange clusters which bloom in the spring.

Distribution

Wiliwili is an endemic plant that is much less common today than in the past. It can be found growing from near the sea shore to about 2,000 ft. in the dry leeward forests and grassy slopes of all the main islands.

Uses

The red seeds of *wiliwili* were strung into *lei*. The light wood was used for surfboards, canoe outriggers and net floats. A proverb says sharks bite when the *wiliwili* flowers.

Silk Oak, Silver Oak, He Oak (R)
'Oka kilika, Ha'ikū ke'oke'o
Grevillea robusta
Family: Proteaceae

Description

The silk oak is a fast-growing tree from Australia that was purposely introduced into the Hawaiian forest as a potential timber resource. Generally, it grows straight and tall, up to 60 ft. or more. Leaves are divided several times. The yellow flowers are interesting and attractive like those of many species in the Protea family. Fruit are brown leather-like capsules. The flowering season lasts from April into fall.

Distribution

Silk oak was introduced to Hawai'i about 1880. Over 2 million silk oaks were planted for timber in Hawai`i between 1919 and 1959. Now naturalized in several forest areas here, silk oak is adapted to semiarid as well as moderately moist mountain regions. Another tree protea (*Grevillea banksii*), is also now naturalized in parts of Hawai'i. It is slender, up to 25 ft. tall, with erect red, yellowish, nearly white or sometimes greenish flowers.

'Iliahi (E)   *Santalum* spp.
Sandalwood   Family: Santalaceae

Description

The native sandalwoods are partly parasitic, small shrubs or trees up to 50 ft. tall. Flowers are four or five parted in various colors (greenish-yellow, orange, pale-red, or magenta). Leaves tend to be small, thick, and pale green or pinkish. Fruits are fleshy, juicy, 1/4 to 1 inch long, reddish or purple to bluish black, and have a distinct ring near the tip.

Distribution and Uses

Species in the sandalwood genus *Santalum* can be found in India, East Malaysia, Australia, and several Pacific islands. Of the total 25 *Santalum* spp., 4 are endemic to Hawai'i, where they are all known as *'iliahi*. Hawaiian sandalwoods occur in dry areas (*S. ellipticum),* moderately wet forests (*S. freycinetianum*), the higher, sub-alpine zone on Haleakalā volcano, Maui (*S. haleakalae*), or only on Hawai'i Island (*S. paniculatum*). Although they used to be abundant in many regions of the Hawai'i, the distribution of these valuable plants is now limited or severely threatened in various areas. Traditionally, *'iliahi* was used in medicines and to scent coconut oil. During the late 18th and early 19th centuries, the aromatic heartwood of these trees was harvested in great quantity and shipped to China where it was used to make incense and fine furniture. The intense sandalwood trade in Hawai'i was an early economic activity that adversely affected both the natural environment and the human population. Today, sandalwood is still one of the world's most valuable natural products.

Koali 'awa (I)   *Ipomoea indica*
Morning Glory   Family: Convolvulaceae

Description

Koali 'awa is a tough, perennial vine with many-branched stems, often more than 25 ft. long, that twine up and over shrubs and small trees. It can form a dense carpet with its 3-4 inch long, heart-shaped leaves. The delicate, blue to purple, or rarely white, funnel-shaped flowers are 2-3 inches long and 2-3 inches wide at the tip. Fruits are small, brown, spherical to flattened capsules.

Distribution

This common, indigenous, pantropical morning glory vine prefers relatively dry, disturbed habitats, exposed to strong, intermittent sunshine. It occurs in Hawai'i from near sea level to over 1,500 ft. elevation.

Uses

Hawaiians have used the bitter-tasting, pounded stems and roots of *koali 'awa* for medicine to relieve aches, pain, and constipation. However, hikers should beware of ingesting any portion of this plant for it may have a dangerous cathartic effect! In fact, hikers should not eat any plant substance without strict confidence that they will not suffer an adverse reaction. Be safe and consult an expert first.

Pāmakani, Pāmakani haole (R)

Ageratina spp.
Family: Asteraceae

Description and Distribution

These alien, weedy herbs (*Ageratina adenophora* and *A. riparia*, the latter is shown above) are 2-4ft tall. They produce leaves 2-4 inches long with serrated margins. Flower heads are small and white (*A. adenophora* is ill-smelling, more erect, somewhat taller, often purplish, and has wider leaves). Introduced from Mexico as potential ornamentals, these plants have escaped cultivation and become naturalized in some moderately wet areas of Hawai'i, especially in disturbed, open places.

Kāhili ginger, *'Awapuhi kāhili* (R)

Hedychium gardnerianum
Family: Zingiberaceae

Description and Distribution

Kāhili ginger is a coarse herb, up to 6 ft. tall or more, with erect, cylindrical, yellow-petalled flowers. No ginger species is native to Hawai'i. The one shown here is native to Asia and cultivated as an ornamental in many tropical areas, including Hawai'i. Its seeds are spread by birds; and thus, it is now a serious weed problem in some areas of Hawai'i. Red Ginger, *'awapuhi 'ula'ula* (*Alpina purpurata*), is shown on page 1; it is now also naturalized in some areas of the Hawaiian Islands.

Montbretia (R)
Crocosmia x crocosmiiflora
Family: Iridaceae

Description
Montbretia is an alien herb in the Iris family. Its leaves are 15-20 inches long and relatively narrow. The bright yellow-orange flowers have a curved tube with spreading or erect oblong segments (flower petals) up to an inch long. The plant produces brown seeds which are wrinkled but not viable.

Distribution
This attractive, introduced ornamental plant is a sterile hybrid of *Crocosmia pottsii* and *C. aurea*, two species which are native to South Africa. Montbretia spreads only by vegetative reproduction, sending out underground, bulb-like stems which develop new shoots. It is a weed in some of the cooler mountain regions on Kaua'i, O'ahu, Maui, and Hawai'i.

Malayan Ground Orchid (R)
Spathoglottis plicata
Family: Orchidaceae

Description
Also known as the Philippine ground orchid, this 1-4 ft. tall alien species has long, folded leaves 1-3 inches wide. It bears dark purple, pinkish, or white flowers on erect stalks. Green, hanging fruit capsules hold a multitude of tiny seeds.

Distribution
A native of S.E. Asia and a few Pacific islands, this introduced orchid is usually found among grasses and ferns in open, disturbed places in moderately wet, lower mountain areas. There are 3 other alien orchid species growing wild in Hawai'i. In addition, 3 native endemic orchid species occur Hawai'i; but these native orchids are not common in most forests.

Liliko'i (R)
Passion Fruit

Passiflora edulis
Family: Passifloraceae

Description and Distribution

The Hawaiian name of the passion fruit (*liliko'i*) is said to honor the place on Maui where it was reportedly first cultivated. This alien woody vine (liana) has grooved stems and large, shiny, lobed leaves. Flowers are white petaled, complex, and attractive. There are 2 forms of the species: f. *edulis* with mature green or greenish purple fruit; and f. *flavicarpa* with mature yellow to reddish fruit. Form *flavicarpa* was introduced in 1923 for its better tasting succulent seed coat (used in desserts and beverages). *Liliko'i* grows wild in some moderately wet forests and shrublands (c. 200-3,500 ft.) on Kaua'i, O'ahu, Lāna'i, Maui, and Hawai'i. There are about 430 species in the genus *Passiflora*. Although none of these vines are native to Hawai'i, 10 or more are now naturalized in these islands. Some are serious pests (see banana poka, below).

Banana *Poka* (R)
Passiflora mollissima
Family: Passifloraceae

Description and Distribution

This alien woody climber is native to the Andes Mts. of South America where farmers cultivate the liana for its edible fruit. It produces wide leaves up to 6 inches long with 3 lobes. It bears large attractive, pink flowers, and soft, yellow, elongated fruits, which look somewhat like bananas. In Hawaiian, *poka* (like *moka*) means offal, waste material, or filth. Banana *poka* is a very serious pest in the moderately wet forests on the islands of Hawai'i and Kaua'i, where it grows up over, and sometimes smothers native plants. Its edible fruit is dispersed by wild pigs and other animals, including humans. It is said to have been first introduced on Hawai'i Island early in this century to cover up an outhouse. Although its appealing foliage and flowers are sometimes used for decorative purposes, people should be especially careful not to spread this extremely aggressive weedy plant!

Glory-Bush, Lasiandra (R)

Tibouchina urvilleana
Family: Melastomataceae

Description
The glory-bush is a 5-12 ft. shrub with brittle stems. It produces hairy, oval leaves, 2-5 inches long with 5-7 longitudinal veins that come to a point at the tip. The abundant flowers have 5 attractive pink or purple petals, 1-2 inches long.

Distribution
A native of southern Brazil, the glory-bush is an ornamental; but like several members of the Melastome family (e.g., *Clidemia hirta*, see below), it can escape from cultivation and become a weed. The glory-bush is now naturalized in some areas on Kaua'i, O'ahu, Maui, and Hawai'i. Another melastome which should definely be kept out of, or removed from, Hawai'i is *Miconia calvescens*, a very aggressive tree which was introduced in Tahiti in 1937. Over 60% of that island is now heavily invaded with dark groves of *Miconia* trees; and as result, many native species there are now threatened with extinction.

Koster's Curse (R)

Clidemia hirta
Family: Melastomataceae

This noxious, alien shrub (2-10 ft. tall) from the Neotropics (Western Hemisphere) is now a widespread weed in the Paleotropics (Eastern Hemisphere). In the Hawaiian Islands, it was first observed in 1941, and since then has become a serious pest in the mountains of O'ahu. It is also found on Kaua'i, Moloka'i, and Hawai'i where it may develop into a significant problem if not controlled in the future. Each of its hairy fruits contain many seeds. Hikers should carefully clean their boots after trekking in areas where *Clidemia* is found!

Thimbleberry or Mauritius Raspberry (R)

Rubus rosifolius
Family: Rosaceae

Description

The thimbleberry or Mauritius raspberry is a small shrub with prickly stems that stand erect, arch above the ground, or spread out as much as 5 to 7 ft. from the root stock. The pinnately compound leaves are 3 inches long with 5 to 7 serrated leaflets up to 4 inches long. Flowers have bright white petals less than an inch long. Fruits are reddish and 1/2 to 1 inch long, and easily detached from the receptacle.

Distribution

Thimbleberry is a member of the raspberry or blackberry genus *Rubus*, which includes about 250 species mainly native to the northern termperate regions and the Andes Mountains of South America. Thimbleberry is native to Asia, but is now naturalized in many tropical areas. This weedy, alien raspberry is said to have been introduced to Hawai'i from Jamaica in the 1880s. Since then it has been dispersed widely throughout the moderately wet and more moist forests of all the main Hawaiian Islands except Ni'ihau and Kaho'olawe. It occurs from near sea level to above 4,000 ft., especially in disturbed places. The thimbleberry produces its appealing edible fruit throughout most of the year, unlike its relative, the prickly Florida blackberry (*Rubus argutus*), an extremely serious alien weed which is now naturalized in a variety of disturbed Hawaiian habitats,

Uses

The fruit of the wild thimbleberry is juicy and rather tasty. Hikers often make a bee-line for the ripe fruit; however, when doing so, they run the risk of getting scratched by the abundant prickles of this alien plant.

Paperbark (R)

Melaleuca quinquenervia
Family: Myrtaceae

Description

A paperbark tree can grow to be about 60-80 feet tall. It is easily recognized by its many-layered, peeling, spongy bark. Leaves tend to be oblong and 2-8 inches long. The cylindrical spikes of whitish flowers are 2-6 inches long and are usually produced at the branch tips with small spherical or hemispherical capsules found below the flowers.

Distribution

Paperbark is native to eastern Australia, New Guinea, and New Caledonia. It was introduced to Hawai'i and planted widely for reforestation purposes, especially in the dry to moderately moist forests. In parts of Florida it is a serious, alien weedy pest.

Uses

In other areas of the world, an oil extracted from paperbark leaves is a valuable source of external medicine for rheumatism and skin disorders. The wood is also valuable for fuel and building purposes. Its special bark provides fire protection for the plant.

Firetree (R)

Myrica faya
Family: Myricaceae

Description

The firetree grows up to heights of 30 ft. or more. Leaves are shiny, dark-green, and 2-4 inches long. Fruits are small, dark red to blackish when mature, and grouped in clusters.

Distribution

This alien, evergreen plant is native to some Atlantic Ocean islands. It was brought to Hawai'i as an ornamental early in this century, most likely by Portuguese immigrants, who made a wine from its fruit. The firetree has escaped from cultivation and is now a serious pest in many forest areas.

Swamp Mahogany (R)

Eucalyptus robusta
Family: Myrtaceae

Description

Swamp mahogany is one of the taller and larger alien trees in the Hawaiian forest. It produces long, narrow, pointed leaves about 2 inches in width, small whitish flowers with many stamens, and cylindrical fruit about 1/2 inch long. The bark is reddish brown, rough, soft, and spongy. This species of *Eucalyptus* grows rapidly, even regenerating from stumps. Its roots are relatively shallow and thus it may be blown over in a strong storm or hurricane.

Distribution and Uses

There are approximately 600 species of *Eucalyptus*. All but 2 are native to Australia. Many are economically important for reforestation, ornament, timber, tannin, and essential oils. More than 90 species of *Eucalyptus* have been introduced to Hawai'i, most for watershed protection. Often planted as a windbreak, swamp mahogany is the most abundant timber tree in the Hawaiian Islands today. Parts of Nānākuli Valley and the Wai'anae coast of O'ahu are shown in the photograph below.

Pāpala kēpau **(E), (I)**   *Pisonia* spp.
Family: Nyctaginaceae

Description and Distribution

These trees or large shrubs, in the four-o'clock family, have soft, brittle wood. They produce clusters of small whitish, greenish, or brownish flowers and elongated, sticky fruits. There are 5 native species of *Pāpala kēpau* in Hawai'i (3 indigenous and 2 endemic). Four of these are found in mountain forests from the lower slopes up to about 4,000 ft., often in gulches. They vary in their adaptation to moisture; for example *Pisonia brunoniana* and *P. sandwicensis* are usually found in dry to moderately wet areas, while *P. umbellifera* is found in more moist areas of the Hawaiian Islands.

Uses

The sticky gum (*kēpau*) that forms on the exterior of the fruit was collected and smeared on the limbs of certain trees to catch birds in ancient Hawai'i. Attractive feathers extracted from the trapped birds were woven into special capes and headdresses. These royal emblems were worn exclusively by the Hawaiian chiefs.

Pāpala **(E)**   *Charpentiera* spp.
Family: Amaranthaceae

Description Distribution

These small trees in the Amaranth Family, up to 35 ft. tall, produce druping slender clusters of tiny flowers and extremely light, flammable dry wood. There are 6 species in the genus *Charpentiera*. One species is found in the Austral and Cook Islands; the other five are endemic to Hawai'i, adapted to moderately wet or more moist forest conditions. The species shown here is *Charpentiera elliptica*.

Uses

The combustible wood of *pāpala* was formerly used by Hawaiians along the north coast of Kaua'i in a fireworks sport called *'ōahi*. Burning pieces of the light wood of this tree were flung from the steep cliffs. The central core of a *pāpala* branch has a soft pith which burns rapidly and emits sparks that discharge like blazing rockets. People riding in canoes in the sea below the cliffs who caught the sparking embers of this wood might brand themselves as a mark of honor.

Māmaki, Māmake (E)

Pipturus spp.
Family: Urticaceae

Description and Distribution

There are 4 endemic species of *Pipturus* in Hawai'i. Leaves are generally ovate, light green underneath, and have prominent veins. Stems bear whitish, fleshy fruit. *Pipturus albidus* is a common, variable shrub or small tree, 6-20 ft. tall, found in moderately wet areas (200-6,000 ft.) on all main islands except Ni'ihau and Kaho'olawe. *Pipturus forbesii* is only found on E. Maui in montane forest and subalpine shrubland (4,500-6,000 ft.). *Pipturus kauaiensis* and *Pipturus ruber* are only found on Kaua'i in moderately wet forests up to about 4,000 ft. Birds eat the fruits and disperse the seeds of these woody plants.

Uses

In ancient Hawai'i, the fruits of *māmaki* were used as a laxative and thrush remedy. Bark and young leaves were also used in traditional medicine. The long, strong fibers of the inner bark provided a cordage material. These fibers were also used to make *kapa* cloth similar to, but coarser, than that of *wauke* (*Broussonetia papyrifera*), the Polynesian introduced paper mulberry plant.

Kukui (P)   *Aleurites moluccana*
Candlenut Tree   Family: Euphorbiaceae

Description

Kukui can develop into a large, spreading tree, reaching heights of 70 ft. or more. Leaves are pale green and quite variable in shape. Flowers are numerous, small, and white. They are produced in clusters at the end of the branches. Fruits are spherical, about 2 inches wide, and have 4 shallow furrows. The hard, dark nuts are over an inch in diameter.

Distribution and Uses

This very useful species in the spurge family is probably native to Southeast Asia; but its exact homeland is difficult to determine because it has been spread by humans to many tropical areas. It was brought to the Hawaiian Islands by the early Polynesian voyagers, and is now naturalized in lower mountain areas of all the major Hawaiian Islands, mainly in dry and wet gulches. Its light green foliage can be easily sighted from a distance (see top left photograph showing *kukui* trees near a stream in Waimea Canyon on Kaua'i). Officially named the State Tree of Hawai'i in 1959, *kukui* has been a valuable plant for centuries. The ancient Hawaiians used the flowers, nuts, and bark medicinally for general exhaustion, asthma, sores, ulcers, swollen womb, and constipation. The flowers and polished nuts were also woven into garlands (*lei*), while the bark and acrid juice of the fleshy nut were used as a dye for tatoos (*tatau*), canoe paint, bark cloth (*kapa*), and fish nets. In addition, the nuts were strung together and burned as a light source, roasted and mashed to make a spicy condiment mixed with salt (*'inamona*), and pressed for a useful oil. The wood was also used for making canoes and fish net floats.

'Uki'uki (I)
Dianella sandwicensis
Family: Liliaceae

Description
'Uki'uki is a perennial herb 2-5 ft. tall. The leaves are strong, but flexible, 1-3 ft. long and about 1 inch wide, with a pronounced midrib. The small, pale blue to white flowers are produced in open clusters. The berries are drooping, blue to purplish, and variable in shape.

Distribution
This native Hawaiian member of the lily family is also a native species in the Marquesas Islands. Therefore botanists refer to it as indigenous (rather than endemic) to Hawai'i. It grows in open to partially shaded areas of moderately wet forest and dry shrubland from about 400-6,500 ft. elevation on all the main Hawaiian Islands except Ni'ihau and Kaho'olawe.

Uses
The extracted juice of the *'uki'uki* fruit was used as a *kapa* cloth dye. The Hawaiians also sometimes used the leaves for thatching their houses. The scientific name of genus *Dianella* originates from Diana, the mythological Roman goddess of chastity, hunting, and the moon; *ella* refers to smallness or affection.

Maile (E)
Alyxia oliviformis
Family: Apocynaceae

Description, Distribution, and Uses

This endemic native twining vine or shrub produces smooth leathery leaves, small yellowish flowers, and 1/2 inch long fruits resembling olives. Plant form, leaf size and shape, and scent vary in *maile*. Varietal names in Hawai'i include: *maile ha'i wale* (brittle *maile*); *maile lau li'i* (small-leaved *maile*); *maile lau nui* (big-leaved *maile*); *maile kaluhea* (sweet *maile*); and *maile pākaha* (blunt-leaved *maile*). All the *maile* plants belong to a single endemic species that grows up and around other plants in the dry to wet forests as high as about 6,000 ft. elevation. The fragrant stem bark and shiny leaves of the beloved *maile* are a favored source of festive, open-ended *lei*. Many songs, chants, and hula compositions were inspired by this sweet-scented plant. Both royalty and the commoners of old Hawai'i enjoyed *maile*, which they dedicated to the hula goddess, Laka.

`Ōhi`a hā (E)
Syzygium sandwicensis
Family: Myrtaceae

Description, Distribution, and Uses

'Ohi'a hā (known as *pā'ihi* on Maui), is an endemic native tree, 10-80 ft. tall, with shredded, grayish to reddish brown bark. It produces inverted, ovate leaves 2-4 inches long. The small, white to pinkish, pompom-like flowers are small and clustered in the axils of the upper leaves. Hikers should spot the abundant fruit which are pink to red when ripe, more or less spherical, and about 1/2 inch wide. Related to native *'ōhi'a lehua* (*Metrosideros* spp.) and the Polynesian introduced *'ōhi'a 'ai* or mountain apple (*Syzygium malaccense*), *'ōhi'a 'hā* can be found on ridges and in sloping areas of the moderately wet to moist forests and bogs, 700-3,500 ft. elevation, on Kaua'i, O'ahu, Moloka'i, Lānai, and Maui. Although somewhat lacking in taste, the small, fleshy pulp of the fruit is edible. The wood of *'ōhi'a hā* was used in house construction and for fuel; and the bark was used in the preparation of a black dye for bark cloth.

Naupaka-Kuahiwi
Mountain Naupaka

Scaevola spp.
Family: Goodeniaceae

Description

There are six endemic species of *Scaevola* in the mountains of Hawai'i. None of them have evolved directly from their common relative, the indigenous beach plant *naupaka kahakai* (*Scaevola sericea*), which is found on many tropical Pacific shores. The *naupaka kuahiwi* shrubs produce white, yellowish, or purplish "half" flowers (5 petals) and roundish, purple fruits. See also *'ohe naupaka* (*Scaevola glabra*) on page 62.

Distribution

The species of *naupaka kuahiwi* shown here (*S. gaudichaudiana*) is common in more open areas of the wet forest, between approximately 500-2,500 ft. elevation on Kaua'i and O'ahu. In the bottom right photograph it is shown underneath a small *'ōhi'a lehua* tree (*Metrosideros* sp.) in the Wai'anae Mts.

Uses

Although the Hawaiians do not seem to have found much use for *naupaka kuahiwi*, they referred to the flowers of these plants in legend. According to one story, the flowers were torn into its present "half" shape by a Hawaiian maiden who believed her lover had been unfaithful. She demanded that he prove his fidelity by finding another whole flower. Unfortunately, he was unsuccessful and was said to have died of a broken heart. Some say the fruits of *naupaka kuahiwi* were used to make a traditional Hawaiian dye.

Koa (E)
Acacia Koa
Family: Fabaceae

Description

This native Hawaiian tree has many forms. In deep, fertile soils it may grow to heights of 100 ft., with huge trunks as wide as 10 ft. in diameter. On poorer soils, scrubby *koa* trees may be much smaller. The flowers are pale-yellowish, globular clusters about 1/2 inch wide. The sickle-shaped foliage is not made up of true leaves but rather of enlarged, flattened petioles or stalks which ordinarily connect the leaf to the stems and branches. *Acacia koa*, endemic to Hawai'i, is closely related to a very similar species (*Acacia heterophylla*) found in the Mascarene Islands of the Indian Ocean.

Distribution

Koa trees are normally found growing in well drained soil in moderately wet forest areas. They occur in open groves on mountain slopes below and above the wetter rain forests on all main islands except Ni'ihau and Kaho'olawe. Although *koa* does regenerate from roots exposed by erosion, the widespread grazing of wild and domesticated cattle, goats, and sheep has greatly reduced the distribution of this majestic native species. Some botanists believe that *koai'e* or *koai'a* (*Acacia koaia*), is a separate native species; compared to *koa*, it is smaller, has narrower leaves, the seeds are arranged vertically in the pod, and its wood is harder. Although the gnarly *koai'e* tree is not common, it is found in drier, open areas of Moloka'i, Lāna'i Maui, and Hawai'i.

Uses

In old Hawai'i, specialized craftsmen (*kahuna*) would locate the large, straight-growing *koa* trees. After an elaborate ritual, the trunks were cut and made into canoes, as well as house beams, carrying sticks, and surfboards. *Koai'e* was used to make spears and fancy paddles. Today highly esteemed *koa* wood is used to make fine furniture.

'Ie'ie (I)   *Freycinetia arborea*
Family: Pandanaceae

Description

This native woody climber (liana) spreads out over the forest floor, often sprawling over rocks. It is frequently found wrapped up around the trunks of the taller trees, especially *'ōhi'a* (*Metrosideros* spp.) and *koa* (*Acacia koa*). *'Ie'ie* stems, roughly an inch in diameter produce many short, or sometime long, wiry, clasping, aerial roots (*'ie*) which attach the plant to a host tree. During the flowering phase, 2-5 bright orange, male and female flowering spikes develop out of the center of the terminal leaf clusters. The spikes are surrounded by leafy bracts which are orange or green with orange bases. Introduced birds (e.g., the Japanese White-eye or mejiro, *Zosterops japonicus*) now pollinate *'ie'ie*; in the past, this was done by native honeycreeper birds (drepanids) that have become extinct.

Distribution

'Ie'ie can be found in most of the lower to medium elevation Hawaiian forest areas (1,000-4,500 ft.), especially where *'ōhi'a*, *koa*, and *kukui* trees are found. This liana often forms a dense, almost impenetrable thicket. In Hawai'i, it has been recorded from all the main islands, except for Ni'ihau and Kaho'olawe. It is also found on several other Pacific islands, and thus is classified as indigenous in Hawai'i.

Uses

'Ie'ie was a sacred plant in old Hawai'i. Dedicated to the forest god Ku, people used the aerial roots and pounded fibers of the stems for constructing houses, outrigger canoes, fish traps, sandals, and wicker frameworks for feather-studded idols and helmets. Flowering branches of *'ie'ie* were used for decorative purposes around altars and fruits were eaten by the early Polynesians as a famine food.

***Manono* (E)**   *Hedyotis terminalis*
                                    Family: Rubiaceae

Description

There is great variation in almost all parts of this species, known in Hawaiian as *manono*. Among the native Hawaiian flowering plants, only *'ōhi'a lehua* (*Metrosideros polymorpha*) probably has more diversity in plant form. *Hedyotis terminalis* (formerly *Gouldia terminalis*) is an endemic shrub, woody vine (liana), or small tree in the Coffee Family, growing up to about 15 ft. in height. *Manono* produces small yellowish green to purple-tinged flowers and clusters of dark blue to purple-black fruits about 1/4 inch in diameter.

Distribution

Unique to Hawai'i, *manono* plants are found in moderately wet to more humid forests. They also occur occasionally in shrubby areas, or even in bog environments from about 800 to 6,000 ft. above sea level on all of the main islands except Ni'ihau and Kaho'olawe.

Uses

The woody parts of *manono* plants were used by the ancient Hawaiians as material for trimming and rigging features on their outrigger canoes.

'Ohelo (E)

Vaccinium spp.
Family: Ericaceae

Description

There are at least 3 endemic species of *Vaccinium* in Hawai'i, all known as *'ōhelo*. Two species, *V. dentatum* (*'ōhelo*) and *V. reticulatum* (*'ōhelo'ai*), are small shrubs; the other species, *V. calycinum* (*'ōhelo kau la'au*), can grow to heights of about 15 ft. Fruits of all 3 species are red (or sometimes yellow, orange, or purplish in *V. reticulatum*) 1/4 to 1/2 inches in diameter, and contain numerous small seeds. Leaves vary in form and are sometimes bright red, as shown in the photograph below of *V. reticulatum* on a lava flow.

Distribution

The genus *Vaccinium* contains about 450 species located in numerous temperate, subtropical, and tropical areas of the world including many Pacific islands. All 3 Hawaiian species of *'ōhelo* can be found in wet forest or bog habitats usually from about 1,500 ft. to 3-4,000 ft.; *'ōhelo 'ai*, which has the tastiest fruit, is most often found in open areas, up to 11,000 ft. or more on the tallest volcanic mountains of the Hawaiian Islands.

Uses

The *'ōhelo* plants are related to huckleberries, blueberries, and cranberries. The fruits are edible raw or cooked into pies and jellies. Dried leaves of *'ōhelo* are still utilized to make a tea. The offering of fruiting branches of *'ōhelo* to the fire goddess, Pele, in the volcano area of Kilauea is a traditional Hawaiian activity to appease this diety.

Ti Plant, *Kī* (P)   *Cordyline fruticosa*
                                                         Family: Agavaceae

Description

The ti plant, *kī* in Hawaiian, is a shrub or small tree that grows from a thick rootstock up to 10 ft. or more. At the ends of the stems, the ti plant produces large, spirally arranged leaves, 1-2 ft. long, and branching clusters of drooping purplish-white flowers. Green-leafed forms of the ti plant rarely produce fruits; reddish-leafed ones bear red berries.

Distribution

The ti plant is a common wild shrub or cultivated plant found in most Pacific Islands and many S.E. Asian areas. It was brought to many Pacific islands and Hawai'i long ago by prehistoric voyagers. It is wide spread in Hawai'i from sea level up to above 3,000 ft. In wilderness areas it is often found along with *kukui* trees (*Aleurites moluccana*) another naturalized species brought to Hawai'i by early Polynesians.

Uses

There are an extraordinary number of traditional utilitarian, ritualistic, and religious uses of this plant throughout much of the tropical Pacific region. Hawaiians have used the ti plant leaves (*la'ī*) for house thatch, temporary skirts, coverings for food, cooking purposes, eating plates, drinking cups, musical instruments, and medicinal potions. The ti plant was also used in many important religious activities. It is still planted around houses because of a strong belief in its protective powers. The swollen roots of the ti plant contain much sugar and were baked and eaten as a famine food and molasses-like confection, which in modern times was distilled into an alcoholic beverage known as *'ōkolehao*.

'Olapa,
Lapalapa (E)
Cheirodendron spp.
Family: Araliaceae

Description

Cheirodendron trees have roundish crowns and compound leaves. Slender stems hold pale green leaflets that flutter (*lapalapa*) in the wind. Small flowers and fruits (purple when mature) are borne in clusters 4-8 inches long.

Distribution

'Ōlapa and *lapalapa* (which has shorter, wider leaflets) are common trees of the wetter Hawaiian forests and bog areas, usually intermixed with tree ferns and *'ōhi'a lehua* (*Metrosideros* spp.). In Hawai'i, there are 5 endemic trees in *Cheirodendron* (a genus in the ginseng family): *C. dominii* is rare; *C. fauriei*, and *C. forbesii* are only found on Kaua'i; *C. platyphyllum* is found on O'ahu and Kaua'i; and *C. trigynum*, the most variable species in this genus, is found on all main islands except Kaho'olawe.

Uses

'Ōlapa was also a Hawaiian word for graceful hula dancers who could imitate the charming movements of the *'ōlapa* leaves waving in the breeze. Poles of *'ōlapa* wood were used to catch birds by smearing them with sticky sap (*kepau*) and placing them in areas where the native birds were abundant. The leaves of *'ōlapa* are woven into a special *lei*. *'Ōlapa* fruit, bark, and leaves yield a bluish-black dye for bark cloth (*kapa*). *Lapalapa* wood was used for fuel, even when still green.

'Ōhi'a lehua (E)
Metrosideros spp.

Family: Myrtaceae

Description

Recent reclassification of the genus *Metrosideros* indicates that there are 5 endemic species in Hawai'i. Among the many Hawaiian names for these plants, *'ōhi'a*, *'ōhi'a lehua*, and *lehua* are the most common. Collectively, these abundant native trees and shrubs are very diverse in form. For example, size, shape, and surface features of the leaves of *Metrosideros* plants differ from individual to individual, as well as from area to area. Four native species usually have attractive reddish, pompom-like flowers; the other (*M. macropus*) almost always has yellowish ones (see p. 43).

Distribution

Closely related to other *Metrosideros* species of some South Pacific Islands and New Zealand, the native Hawaiian species occupy many types of environments from near sea level to over 8,000 ft. elevation.

These woody species can be found as rather small plants in bogs (often in naturally bonsai-like forms), on new lava flows, and on dry cliffs; they also occur in the form of large trees up to 80 ft. tall, growing in deep fertile soils. *'Ōhi'a lehua* may also begin its life cycle as

an epiphyte; i.e., as a plant which grows upon another plant, such as *hāpu'u* (*Cibotium* spp.) tree ferns, but does not derive food or water from the host species. An epiphyte is an "airplant" which obtains its nutrients from the air, rainwater, or organic debris deposited on the host plant. *Metrosideros polymorpha* is the most common Hawaiian species in the genus. It dominates many wet forests, supplying microhabitats for several small ferns, herbs, mosses, liverworts, and lichens that grow on the branches of this widespread tree (see p. 69). Native birds such as the red-feathered *'apapane* can be seen feeding on the nectar-rich blossoms.

Uses

The dark, hard, and long lasting *'ōhi'a* wood was used in canoe making and house construction. In addition, *poi* boards, bowls, and temple carvings were made out of the attractive and durable wood.

'Ohi'a lehua (continued)

The young reddish-crimson leaves (*liko lehua*) are steeped to make a tonic tea. The flowers are said to have been used as an aid in childbirth. Many songs and tales of old Hawai'i refer to the *lehua* flower, which is sacred to the volcano goddess, Pele. According to legend, if someone picks *lehua* flowers on his or her way up into the mountain forest, it will cloud over and the person will be enveloped in a thick mist or rain; but it is permissible to collect the attractive flowers on the way out of the forest. *Lehua* flowers and leaf buds are woven into colorful garlands *(lei)*. The Hawaiian god Kū sometimes took the form of the *'ohi'a lehua* tree, and timber from these trees was used exclusively to make wooden features of complex temples (*heiau*). According to an ancient source, the *'ohi'a* tree had a human voice, and a groan could be heard when it was cut. Another story tells us that the goddess Hina took the form of an *'ohi'a* tree and kept a watch

on a small youth in Waipio Valley. The yellow blossomed *'ohi'a* (*lehua mamo*) shown here was photographed in the Ko'olau Mts., O'ahu. *'Ohi'a lehua* is the special flower of Hawai'i Island. The photograph below shows *'ohi'i lehua* on a lava flow of Kilauea volcano.

Hāpuʻu ʻiʻi, Hāpuʻu pulu, Hāpuʻu, Meu **(E)**   *Cibotium* spp.
Hawaiian Tree Fern   Family: Dicksoniaceae

Description

There are four endemic species of *Cibotium* tree ferns in the Hawaiian Islands: *C. chamissoi* (*Hāpuʻu* or *Meu*), *C. menziesii* (*Hāpuʻu iʻi*), *C. glaucum* (*Hāpuʻu pulu*), and *C. nealiae* (only on Kauai). Some of these large ferns are as tall as 30 ft. Trunks are about 1-3 ft wide and comprise a central stem surrounded by tightly interwoven, dark-colored roots. Under sides of the huge fronds, 6-12 ft. long, produce sori, which are collections of stalked sporangia (spore cases). These contain the minute reproductive bodies.

Distribution

These native tree ferns inhabit shady regions of the wet Hawaiian forests, where they are often very abundant. They require a moist environment and usually are found as an understory of rain forest trees such as *ʻōhiʻa lehua* (*Metrosideros* spp.) and *ʻōlapa* (*Cheirodendron* spp., see the opposite page).

Uses

In ancient Hawaiʻi, the silky bud-hair (soft scales or *pulu*) was used as a an absorbent surgical dressing, and as stuffing for embalming the dead. Also, in times of famine, the pithy starch found in the core of the trunk was baked and eaten. Cut trunks were formerly used to make large bins for cultivating yams (*uhi*). Historically, *pulu* was collected and exported as pillow and mattress stuffing. This activity is now illegal.

Uluhe (I)
False Staghorn Fern

Dicranopteris linearis
Family: Gleicheniaceae

Description
This primitive tropical fern (also known by the genus name *Gleichenia*) has lengthy, creeping stems which fork repeatedly and thus form a thick, often impenetrable, tangle of vegetation. *Uluhe* spreads out by means of underground rootstocks that produce the hard, wiry stems which can grow up to heights of 2-10 ft. above the ground. The yellowish green color of the smooth leaves stands out among the forest vegetation.

Distribution
Uluhe is one of the most common native plants of the wetter Hawaiian forests, usually growing over exposed landslides or artificially disturbed areas in the mountains. Thickets of *uluhe* can smother vegetation and prevent the growth of other plants. In some places it even invades gardens. This fern is also often found in association with *'ōhi'a lehua* (see photograph above). In many other tropical Pacific environments, this fern species also commonly covers areas opened up by natural forces or human activities. When areas covered by this fern become too dry, fire becomes a serious threat.

Uses
In Hawai'i, the bitter juice of *uluhe* stems and leaves was used as a laxative or emetic. On some other tropical Pacific islands, this fern is used to make house thatch. Hikers beware: tall, dense thickets of this fern can be difficult to move through. The sharp, stiff stems pose a hazard to hikers traversing a mass of *uluhe*, which may obscure ditches, or even hide a steep cliff dropoff!

Hulumoa, Kaumahana (E)
Hawaiian Mistletoes
Korthalsella spp.
Family: Viscaceae

Description

Hawaiian mistletoe species are parasitic subshrubs or perennial herbs with flat or cylindrical, jointed, evergreen stems. Leaves are extremely small, and the tiny flowers are clustered in the leaf axils. Perched on host plants, the roots of these parasites penetrate deep enough to draw upon the food supply flowing under the bark of woody plants. This process may seriously injure the host plants.

Distribution

There are 6 native mistletoe species in Hawai'i, 2 indigenous and 4 endemic. They can be found parasitizing several trees and shrubs. Some occur in wet habitats, such as the flat stemmed *Korthalsella latissima*, most common in moist forests on Kaua'i. Others, with narrow rounded stems, are found growing on woody plants in dry to wet areas, e.g., *K. cylindrica* and *K. remyana*.

Wāwae'iole (I)
Lycopodium cernuum
Family: Lycopodiaceae

Description

This primitive club moss is a creeping, evergreen plant with branching stems. It produces tiny, pointed, scale-like leaves and small cones at the tips which curve downward as they mature. The cones resemble rat's feet, hence its Hawaiian name.

Distribution and Uses

Among the *Lycopodium* spp. native to Hawai'i, this *wāwae'iole*, is the most common. It is found in the ground cover of Hawai'i and many other tropical areas, occuring in open or disturbed places, especially in thickets of *uluhe*. Stems of this club moss are used in leis, Christmas wreathes, and flower arrangements. It is said to have been used traditionally in preparing bath water used to treat people suffering from rheumatism.

47

Aloalo (E)
Native Hibiscus Species
Family: Malvaceae

Aloalo is a general Hawaiian name for all kinds of hibiscus plants. Worldwide, there are about 200 species of subshrubs, shrubs, and trees in the diverse *Hibiscus* genus. Four of these species are endemic to Hawai'i, primarily restricted to tropical and subtropical regions. The yellow-flowered plant shown here is *Hibiscus brackenridgei* (Hawaiian name: *ma'o hau hele*). It produces the official State Flower of Hawai'i. This rare, endemic plant is found in some dry forests and shrubland areas on all the main Hawaiian Islands, except Ni'ihau and Kaho'olawe. Two subspecies have been identified: subsp. *brackenridgei*, a sprawling to erect, shrub or small tree found in arid areas from near sea level to more than 1,000 ft. elevation on Moloka'i, Lāna'i, Maui, and Hawai'i; and subsp. *mokuleianus*, a tree also found in arid places, but only in restricted areas

of Kaua`i and the Wai`anac Mts. of O'ahu. The red-flowered plant shown here is *Hibiscus clayi*, an endemic shrub or small tree found in some dry forests on Kaua'i. The form and structure of this woody plant is very similar to that of the endemic *Hibiscus kokio* (Hawaiian names: *koki'o ula*, *aloalo*, *mākū*), which has larger, red, orange, or even yellowish colored petals. Horticulturalists have crossed some of the more attractive forms of the native *Hibiscus kokio* with varieties of the common alien, ornamental, and hedge species *Hibiscus rosa-sinensis* (the Chinese or red hibiscus). Native *Hibiscus kokio* is found in some dry and wet forest areas of Kaua'i, O'ahu, Moloka'i, Maui, and perhaps Hawai'i. *Hibiscus arnottianus* (Hawaiian names: *koki'o ke'oke'o*, *hau hele*, *koki'o kea*, *pāmakani*, and *puaaloalo*, shown on the next page) is found in moist forest areas on O'ahu, and in Wailau Valley, Moloka'i. Traditionally, parts of the native *aloalo* flowers were consumed as a mild laxative for both children and adults.

Koki 'o ke 'oke 'o (E)

Hibiscus arnottianus

Family: Malvaceae

This native white hibiscus grows wild as a shrub or small tree between elevations of c. 1000 to 3,000 ft.

More abundant in the past, *Koki'o-Ke'oke'o* was referred to in several ancient Hawaiian chants and stories. Today it is sometimes cultivated as an ornamental in upland gardens and has often been crossed with other hibiscus species in order to produce decorative varieties.

Kōpiko (E)   *Psychotria* spp.
Family: Rubiaceae

Description

Psychotria, belonging to the coffee family, is a very large genus, including about 1,500 species. Eleven of these species are endemic to Hawai'i; *kōpiko* is the Hawaiian name that refers to most, if not all of these species (*'ōpiko* is a name used on Hawai'i Island). *Kōpiko* plants are large shrubs or small trees that produce thick leathery leaves, small whitish flowers, and fleshy orange fruits about 1/2 inch long.

Distribution and Uses

Common in wet forest environments, *kōpiko* plants can often be found growing in association with *'ōhi'a lehua* (*Metrosideros*) and tree ferns. Some species of *Psychotria* in the Hawaiian Islands have restricted geographical distributions. For example, *P. grandiflora, P. greenwelliae, P. hobdyi,* and *P. wawrae,* are only found on Kaua'i, or a restricted part of that island. *P. fauriei* is only found on or near the windswept summits of the Ko'olau Mts. of O'ahu; *P. hathewayi* is only found in moderately wet or dry forest areas of the Wai'anae Mts. of O'ahu; and although *P. hawaiiensis* is occasionally found on Moloka'i and Maui, it is most common on Hawai'i. The hard, whitish wood of *kōpiko* was formerly used to make anvils for beating bark into *kapa* cloth, and for firewood.

Alani (E)   *Melicope* spp.
Family: Rutaceae

Description

There are many endemic Hawaiian species in the Pacific genus *Melicope* (formerly *Pelea*), with 47 species classified as unique to Hawai'i. These shrubs to small trees produce simple, opposing or whorled leaves. Small yellow flowers and four-parted fruit capsules develop from axillary buds on the branches. Seeds are glossy black when ripe.

Distribution and Uses

The genus *Melicope* belongs to the citrus family. The native species in this genus are widely distributed in Hawai'i from the upper dry forest to the wetter mountain regions, and even into the very humid bogs such as those in the Alaka'i swamp region of Kaua'i. Many species of *Melicope* are known as *alani* (or *alani kuahiwi*) in Hawaiian. There are some exceptions. For example, *Melicope clusiifolia* (shown in the photographs on this page) is known as *kūkaemoa* ("chicken dung"), probably due to the appearance of its "cauliflory" fruit; and beloved, sweet-smelling *Melicope anisata*, only found on Kaua'i, is known as *mokihana*. The light colored wood of *alani* plants was used to make *kapa* beaters and canoe parts. The fragrant leaves of one *alani* (*Melicope sandwicensis*), found only on O'ahu, were used to scent *kapa*. The small, leathery, anise-scented fruits and leaved twigs of *mokihana* are strung into a lei which represents the island of Kaua'i in the leis of the islands.

'Ama'u (E)   *Sadleria* spp.
                         Family: Blechnaceae

Description

'Ama'u is the Hawaiian name for all species of ferns in the endemic genus *Sadleria*. These ferns usually have relatively short trunks, rarely taller than 5 ft. But these plants reach higher with their 2 to 3 ft. long fronds. These fronds change color as they age (from reddish during youth to dark green with maturity). The narrower, smaller, and less divided (less lacy) fronds of 'ama'u ferns differentiate them from the *hāpu'u* (*Cibotium* spp.) tree fern species (see page 44).

Distribution

'Ama'u ferns are commonly found in various sizes and forms where rain forests occur. They can also be found growing in clumps on new lava flows on Hawai'i Island where they are early colonizing species. In addition, these ferns occur in moderately dry rocky gulches and some moun-

tain slopes. Overall, these ferns have a very broad distributional range in elevation from near sea level on some coastal cliffs to about 8,000 ft. in some subalpine regions. *Sadleria cyatheoides* and *Sadleria pallida* ('ama'u 'i'i) are two common species in the genus.

Uses

The *pulu* (soft scales or "hair") of 'ama'u and *hāpu'u* ferns (see page 44) was formerly used as pillow and mattress stuffing. In old Hawai`i, small chunks of a green pulpy paste were taken from the stems of 'ama'u ferns and used as a glue to patch scraps of used barkcloth (*kapa*) together, thus recyling many pieces of old worn clothing. Traditionally, the tasteless pith of these ferns served as a famine food. A red *kapa* dye was made from parts of the plants. In addition, the fronds were used to mulch dryland taro as well as for certain aspects of house thatching and dedication of religious structures (*heiau*). 'Ama'u was associated with Kamapua'a, the pig god, who could take the form of such a fern at will.

Pa'iniu (E)

Astelia spp.
Family: Liliaceae

Description

The native *pa'iniu* plants are small perennial herbs in the lily family with short stems and long, thin, silvery leaves that form rosettes. The flowers are small, greenish-yellow, and borne in clusters. The fruit are small, bright orange, and are produced during the summer.

Distribution

There are 3 endemic species of *pa'iniu*. *Astelia menziesiana* occurs on all main islands except Ni'ihau and Kaho'olawe; the other two species, *A. argyrocoma* and *A. waialealae*, are only found on Kaua'i. These epiphytic plants are usually found growing on the trunks and branches of native trees in wet mountain forests. Birds eat the fruit and thus aid in the dispersal of the seed. The *pa'iniu* plants shown here were photographed near the Alaka'i swamp on the island of Kaua'i.

Uses

Hawaiians wove the silvery skin of these plants into their flower garlands they called *lei pa'iniu*. In historic times, these were often strung around their hats as indication of their visits to the forest areas where the *pa'iniu* plants grow. Occasionally, in ancient times, parts of these herbaceous native plants were used for house thatch.

Pilo (E)
Hupilo

Coprosma spp.
Family: Rubiaceae

Description

In Hawai'i there are several native species in the genus *Coprosma*. Many are known as *pilo*. Both the Hawaiian and scientific names refer to the foul or swampy odor produced by the bruised parts of some plants. These shrubs or small trees have simple, narrow to rounded leaves with smooth margins. The flowering season for these plant is generally at the end of the *ho'oilo* or winter season. The flowers are unisexual and the plants are dioecious (in other words, male and female flowers are segregated on separate plants). The drupe fruits are usually small, fleshy, two-seeded, and yellowish-orange, reddish-orange, bright orange, or black (also see *Kūkaenene, Coprosma ernodeoides,* on page 76).

Distribution

Coprosma is a genus belonging to the coffee family. It contains more than ninety species of shrubs and small trees distributed over many parts of Southeast

Asia and Oceania. Most are native to New Zealand; but several are also found in Australia (8 species), New Guinea (11 species), and Hawai'i (13 species). The other species of *Coprosma* are spread out over a large area of the Indo-Pacific region. The species shown on page 54 are *Coprosma longifolia* (top), with 1/4 inch long fruit, and *Coprosma foliosa* (bottom), with 1/3 inch long fruit. The species shown above on this page are *Coprosma montana*, native to the upper slopes of East Maui and the higher elevations of Hawai'i Island. The male flowers of *Coprosma longifolia* are depicted in the photograph below.

Hō‘awa, Hā‘awa (E)
Pittosporum spp.
Family: Pittosporaceae

Description
These small evergreen trees and shrubs produce shiny leaves that are 4-10 inches long, 1-2.5 inches wide, and more or less grouped at branch tips. The undersides of the leaves often have light brown to dark woolly hairs. The flowers occur in short clusters, usually in leaf axils or along stems. The fruit capsules are rounded, leathery, or woody. They contain two to many dark seeds which stand out against the striking orange or orange-red inner surface of an open capsule. Seeds are set in thick sticky resin and are probably dispersed by birds.

Distribution
There are 12 species of *Pittosporum* growing wild in Hawai‘i, 10 are endemic and 2 are alien, introduced in recent times. The native species are adapted to various environments including dry to wet forests, sub-alpine woodlands, and open bogs up to more than 6,000 ft. elevation. One species, *P. kauaiense*, found only on Kaua‘i, has relatively large leaves and is thus known as *hō‘awa lau nui*.

Uses
Although these plants were considered to be poisonous, according to Neal, the pounded outer layer of the fruit valves of *hō‘awa* were traditionally used to cure sores. In ancient times, the wood of these endemic plants was sometimes used to make gunwales for canoes.

Kōlea (E)

Myrsine spp.
Family: Myrsinaceae

Description and Distribution

These native trees and shrubs have oval to narrow leaves, more or less crowded at branch tips (young leaves may have a distinctive pinkish or reddish hue). Tiny flowers occur in clusters at leaf axils or just below the leaves. Fruits are small, globular, usually numerous, yellow or red to black, and one-seeded. About 20 endemic species of *Myrsine* are found in Hawai'i, distributed over a wide variety of habitats. All evolved apparently from 1 or 2 original ancestral species; and thus, like many species in other genera found in these islands, the native *Myrsine* plants are an excellent example of adaptive radiation.

Uses

The wood of *kōlea* was used in house and canoe construction, as well as to make *kapa* (bark cloth) beaters. *Kapa* dyes were made from these plants; a red one from the wood sap and a black one from the wood charcoal.

Olomea, Pua'a olomea, (E)

Perrottetia sandwicensis
Family: Celastraceae

Description and Distribution

Olomea is an endemic shrub or small tree up to about 20-25 ft. in height with red to green branches. The shiny leaves arc 3-8 inches long with serrated edges. Leaf stems and veins are usually red or reddish orange. Tiny greenish flowers are formed in clusters. Fruit are numerous, small, round, and red. It is common in the understory of wet forests, 1,000-4,000 ft. elevation, on all the main islands except Ni'ihau and Kaho'olawe On Maui, where it is also known as *waimea*, this plant grows up to about 6,000 ft. elevation.

Uses

Olomea was used to make fire in ancient Hawai'i by rotating a piece of its hard wood rapidly against the soft wood of *Hau* (*Hibiscus tiliaceous*). In traditional Hawaiian culture, *olomea* is one of the plant forms of the pig demigod Kamapua'a.

Kāmakahala (E)

Labordia spp.
Family: Loganiaceae

Description

These shrubs or small trees produce paired leaves which are commonly oval with smooth margins and pale green on the lower surface. Known as *kāmakahala*, they are dioecious (i.e., the male and female flowers are segregated on separate plants). The small five-parted, tubular flowers are solitary or clustered at branch tips. Petals are yellow, greenish yellow, or rarely white and fairly thick. Fruits are green or white capsules with many seeds in an orange pulp.

Distribution and Uses

Labordia, in Loganiaceae, the strychnine family, is a genus endemic to Hawai'i. Therefore, all 16 of the species belonging to this genus are only found in Hawai'i. Theoretically evolving from a single ancestor, these species are another fine example of adaptive radiation in Hawai'i. They are usually found in damp, shady forest between 1,000-5,000 ft. elevation. One species, *Labordia waialealae,* with leaves only 1 inch long or less, is known as *kāmakahala lau li'i*, "small-leafed *kāmakahala*." The two species shown here are *L. hedyosmifolia* (top left) and *L. hosakana* (below). According to Hillebrand (1888), the flowers of three *Labordia* species he described were so highly esteemed that they were used in garlands and wreaths reserved for the high chiefs only and forbidden to the common people.

Hoi kuahiwi (E)
Smilax melastomifolia
Family: Smilacaeae

Description

Hoi kuahiwi (also known as *aka'awa*, and *pi'oi* on Kaua'i) is an endemic woody climber. The tuberous rhizomes of this native vine produce finely grooved stems which are smooth or bear few to many short, cone-shaped prickles. The shiny, normally pointed leaves vary in form, but are most often heart-shaped, 2 to 7 inches long and 2 to 8 inches wide, with 5 to 7 conspicuous longitudinal veins. Leaves are arranged alternately on the stems. Two tendrils arise from the base of the twisted, half inch long leaf stalk (petiole). Like other members of the genus *Smilax*, this native species is dioecious, with the small male and female flowers segregated on separate plants (see male flowers in bottom right photograph). Flowers are borne in round clusters at leaf axils. Fruits are globular berries less than a half inch long.

Distribution and Uses

There are about 300 species in the genus *Smilax*, known in English as "catbrier" and "greenbrier." Only one is found in Hawai'i. It occurs in moist wooded areas and margins of bogs, up to 6,000 ft. *Hoi kuahiwi* (which means "mountain yam" in Hawaiian) is not a true yam species, but it does resembles *hoi*, the alien "bitter yam" or "poison yam" vine (*Dioscorea bulbifera*). *Hoi*, a true yam species, was brought to Hawai'i by early Polynesians and introduced into forested areas; it still grows wild in some places. Underground and aerial tubers (*'ala'ala*) of the wild alien yam are poisonous. However, the underground tubers were eaten in times of famine if they were properly prepared, which included lengthy cooking and repeated washing with water. According to W.F. Hillebrand (1888), early Hawaiians also ate the tuberous root of the native *Smilax* vine, *hoi kuahiwi*, during times of extreme food scarcity. Sasparilla, a widely used flavoring, is extracted from a few tropical American relatives of *hoi kuahiwi*.

'*Ākala* (E)
Hawaiian Raspberry

Rubus spp.
Family: Rosaceae

Description

Native *'ākala* plants belong to the large raspberry genus *Rubus* which includes about 250 species of erect or low lying shrubs with prickles. Hawai'i has 2 endemic species, *R. hawaiensis* with large erect stems, 5 to 15 ft. tall and *R. macraei* with low lying stems. Unlike other raspberry species, Hawaiian raspberries produce small, rather weak prickles. Both native species are known as *'ākala*. Leaves are palmately compound and serrated. Flowers petals are dark pink to dusky rose or occasionally white in *R. hawaiensis*. The edible fruits are dark red to dark purple, sometimes yellow in *R. hawaiensis*, and juicy in *R. macraei*.

Distribution and Uses

'Ākala plants are now relatively rare. The weakly-prickled native raspberries are susceptible to the impact of alien hoofed mammals such as goats, sheep, and cattle. These herbivores were introduced in historic times (since 1778). Many escaped into forested areas where their pressure on numerous, vulnerable native species has drastically reduced many endemic plants to rare or endangered status. *Rubus hawaiensis* is found in moist forest between 2,000-6,500 ft. on Kaua'i, Moloka'i, Maui, and Hawai'i. *Rubus macraei* is found between 5,000-6,500 ft. on East Maui and Hawai'i. *'Ākala* fruit are ripe from April to July and vary in taste. Ashes from burnt plant material were used for scaly scalp, heartburn, and vomiting. Dark dye was extracted from the fruit and a pink dye from the flowers.

Kanawao (E)
Pū'ahanui
Broussaisia arguta
Family: Hydrangeaceae

Description

Kanawao (also known as *pū'ahanui*) is a thickly branched, native shrub, 5-15 ft. tall in the saxifrage family. This unique native species is a relative of the garden ornamental hydrangea. It is the only member of the endemic Hawaiian genus *Broussaisia*. The plant produces large, serrated leaves, 4-16 inches long. Flowers are unisexual, and the plants seem to be dioecious, producing attractive, convex clusters of small white (*kanawao ke'oke'o*) to pinkish-purple (*kanawao 'ula'ula*), or even bluish-green flower petals. The fruits are red to maroon, about 1/3 inch wide, and contain numerous tiny seeds.

Distribution and Uses

Kanawao is common in many of the more moist Hawaiian forests. It is often found in association with *'ōhi'a* (*Metrosideros* spp.) and *'ōlapa* (*Cheirodendron* spp.) between about 1,500 and 4,500 ft. elevation on all main islands except Ni'ihau and Kaho'olawe. The fruits of these plants were believed to increase fecundity, and therefore were sometimes used to aid in the act of conception. An expansion in the number of chiefs in traditional Hawai'i was compared to a multi-fruit cluster of the *kanawao* plant.

'Ohe naupaka (E)
Scaevola glabra
Family: Goodeniaceae

Description

This endemic woody species was formerly classified in the genus *Camphusia*. More recently, botanists have assigned it to *Scaevola*, the genus which also includes six endemic Hawaiian species known as *naupaka kuahiwi* (see page 35); but genetic and plant chemistry evidence suggests that *'ohe naupaka* evolved from an different ancestoral species than the *naupaka kuahiwi* species of Hawai'i. Compared to the *naupaka kuahiwi* species, *'ohe naupaka* produces tougher leaves, which are smooth, 2 to 6 inches long, 1 to 2 inches wide, and more or less crowded near the ends of the branches. One, or occasionally two, erect or hanging flowers are borne in the leaf axils. They are bright yellow, waxy, curved, tubular, and about 1 inch long.The fruits are dark purplish black and about 1/2 inch long. Usually developing into a shrub, 5-15 ft. tall, under some ecological conditions this species may produce a tree-like individual with a trunk approaching one foot in diameter.

Distribution

'Ohe naupaka is found only in wet forests, 600-2,500 ft, on the islands of Kaua'i and in the Ko'olau Mts. of O'ahu. This species may have evolved into its particular ecological niche in the moist Hawaiian forests earlier than other *naupaka* species. *'Ohe naupaka* has long curved flowers, somewhat similar to the native lobeliad plants (see pages 63-65), The shape of these flowers seems to be an evolutionary adaptation to pollination by some of the unique, long, curve-beaked, endemic Hawaiian honeycreeper birds (Drepanids). The birds sip the nectar produced by these native plants, and in the process help fertilize them. Unfortunately, many of these highly specialized, endemic Hawaiian forest birds are now rare, endangered, or extinct. Not only is the loss of these members of the native avifauna sad for the birds themselves, but their disappearance also may threaten the continued existence of those plants they did or do fertilize.

ʻŌhā, Hāhā (E)
Native lobelias
Family: Campanulaceae

Lobelias belong to the bellflower family, which includes 110 endemic Hawaiian species in 7 genera in the subfamily Lobelioidae. All native Hawaiian lobelias probably evolved here from 5 (or less) original colonization events. In Hawaiʻi, under less competitive stress in extreme geographical isolation, and with a wide variety of ecological opportunities, lobelia species evolved in unusual ways through adaptive radiation. In 1888, W.F. Hillebrand called these special native plants the "peculiar pride of our flora." Unfortunately, many of our unique lobelia species are now threatened with extinction because of the intense pressure of human land use and the introduction of many noxious alien weeds. Wild grazing animals and rats are also serious threats to many lobelia populations. About 25% of the native lobelia species have disappeared within this century! Hikers should be especially satisfied when sighting these remarkable plants among the forest vegetation.

Description
The native unbranched or sparingly branched lobelias vary in height from 2-40 ft., some developing into shrubs and small trees, others into small, thick-stemmed succulents, such as the species of *Brighamia*. The leaves of these highly variable plants are borne as tufts at the ends of stems and branches. The flowers are produced in diverse colors and shapes, many conspicuously curved and tubular. As suggested on the previous page (*ʻohe naupaka, Scaevola glabra*), the arched flower shape may have co-evolved with some of the long, curved beaks of the native nectar sipping forest birds of Hawaiʻi.

Distribution
The native Hawaiian lobelias are commonly found in the wetter environments, including the very moist bogs; but some, such as the two fleshy, endemic Brighamia species occur on some sea cliffs and steep ridges. Photos on this page show *Clermontia fauriei* (*hāhāʻaiakamanu*) from Kōkeʻe, Kauaʻi.

A native member of the Lobelia family from the Mt. Ka'ala bog region of Oahu.
(Trematolobelia macrostachys)

More Native Lobelias

Hawai'i has 8 genera of Lobelias: 6 endemic, 1 indigenous, and 1 alien (naturalized). The 7 native genera include *Brighamia, Clermontia, Cyanea, Delissea, Lobelia* (indigenous), *Rollandia*, and *Trematolobelia*. The unusual plant shown above is Koli'i, one of four species in the endemic genus *Trematolobelia*. It is somewhat common on O'ahu and Maui, but very rare elsewhere. The bottom left photograph shows *Hāhā lua* (*Cyanea leptostegia*), a palm-like tree lobeliad (10-40 ft. tall), only found in moderately wet forest (3,000-4,000 ft.) in W. Kaua'i. Like several other species in the complex genus *Cyanea*, juvenile leaves of *C. leptostegia* are more deeply lobed or dissected than those of the adult plants. Some biologists believe that the fleshy-fruited lobeliads are descendants of related species native to the Andes Mountains of South America.

Lobelia yuccoides (**E**)

This endemic species, known in Hawaiian as *pānaunau* (top right photograph), grows on dry ridges and canyons in the Wai'anae Mts. of O'ahu and on Kaua'i from about 2,000 to 3,500 ft. Flowers are yellowish to greenish white, curved, tubular, 1.5-2 inches long, with purplish veins. *Pānaunau* means to move up and down. This is what the plant does as its long stems wave in the wind. Pearl Harbor, O'ahu can be seen in the background of the photograph.

Clermontia grandiflora (**E**)

This endemic lobelia shrub in the genus *Clermontia* (bottom photo) grows to heights of 3-20 ft. The suspended, tubular flowers have greenish, purplish, maroon, or rose colored petals. Mature fruits are orange and about 1/2 inch wide. It is found in wet forests and near bogs between 1,600 and 6,000 ft. on the islands of Lāna'i, Maui, and Moloka'i.

Moa (I)

Psilotum nudum
Family: Psilotaceae

Description

This strange, very primitive plant is a living link to the ancient past and earlier forms of the earth's vegetation. *Moa* barely reaches one foot in height. It produces small, slender, forking branches with tiny, pointed, scale-like "leaves." The green parts of the stems above ground actually function as leaves. The underground parts of the stems serve as roots since they contain a very small fungus which absorbs nutrients and water. The three-chambered, yellow fruiting bodies (sporangia) open when ripe and release a multitude of tiny spores.

Distribution and Uses

Found in many tropical environments, *moa* grows on the ground, in rocky crevices, or as an air-plant (epiphyte) perched on the trunks of trees. It can survive in moderately dry as well as wet environments. Traditionally, Hawaiians have prepared a thrush medicine and laxative tea by boiling the *moa* plant. The oily spores were used by men as a kind of talcum powder to prevent groin irritation produced by wearing loin cloths (*malo*), and children played a game with this plant.

'Ala'ala wai nui (E)

Peperomia spp.
Family: Piperaceae

Description

'Ala'ala wai nui is a Hawaiian name for plants in the genus *Peperomia*, which belongs to the pepper family. There are 26 species of *Peperomia* in the Hawaiian Islands; 23 are endemic; 2 are indigenous; and 1 is an alien, now naturalized. These annual or perennial, succulent herbs vary in height from a few inches to 3-4 ft. Tiny flowers are produced on erect stalks.

Distribution and Uses

'Ala'ala wai nui plants are found in various dry to wet environments, growing on the ground or perched on trees and rocks. The sticky fruits are probably dispersed on the feet and feathers of birds. Traditionally in the Hawaiian Islands, these plants have been used in the preparation of many medicinal potions, and to produce a gray *kapa* (bark cloth) dye.

Sundew Plant, *Mikinalo* (I)
Drosera angelica
Family: Droseraceae

Description

This sundew plant, known in Hawaiian as *mikinalo* ("to suck flies"), is a very small, perennial, insectivorous herb. It traps insects that land on the sticky, glandular tentacle hairs of the leaf blades. After these animals becomes stuck to the adhesive leaves, they die, gradually decay, and eventually become absorbed by the plant which uses them to supplement its nutrition.

Distribution

Mikinalo is indigenous to Hawai'i; it is also native to bog environments in the colder areas of the Northern Hemisphere. In Hawai'i, it is only found on Kaua'i where it is common in the mountain bogs. Seeds of this plant probably came to Hawai'i attached to the muddy feet of migrating shorebirds, possibly on the Lesser Golden-Plover (*Pluvialis dominica*), which travels seasonally between northern regions (such as Alaska and Siberia) and the Hawaiian Islands.

Mosses (*Limu*)

Limu is a general Hawaiian name for many forms of algae, as well as lichens, liverworts, and mosses. Mosses grow on trees, rocks, soil, in bogs, or submerged in streams. Widely distributed through the world, mosses occur in high latitude environments as well as near the equator. Some species can be found near the sea shore, while others may be found on high mountain peaks (*limu'ahu'ula*). In Hawai'i there are numerous species of mosses, especially in the rain forests (*limu kele*) where they form a blanket-like cover on some native trees. The next page shows a multitude of small ferns, mosses, and leafy liverworts (more primitive relatives of the mosses) covering the branches of the mossy forest (*limu kau lāau*) growing in the summit bog on Mt. Ka'ala, O'ahu.

Fungi

Most plants obtain their energy through photosynthesis; fungi do not because they lack chlorophyll. Instead, they extract their needs from decaying or dead organisms. Fungi are also referred to as "decomposers." By breaking down organic matter in their life processes, fungi provide a crucial mechanism for the necessary recycling of nutrients in the world's ecosystems. There are many forms of fungi including slime molds, rot, smut, wilt, mushrooms, and bract fungus. The top photograph shows *pepeiao akua*, the edible, fleshy, ear-shaped, tree fungus (*Auricularia* sp.). The bottom photograph shows a bract or shelf fungus. Both fungi are growing on fallen branches of *kukui* (*Aleurites moluccana*).

Hawai'i has many diverse and interesting species of fungi. Most native Hawaiian mushrooms are small and inconspicuous. The prominent stems and caps of mushrooms develop during the reproductive stage of certain fungi. Be very careful when considering whether or not to consume a particular mushroom or other fungi. Some are edible and tasty; others, however, can be harmful. Some mushroom species of *Copelandia* and *Panaeolus* which occur in Hawai'i, often in or near cow dung in pastures, contain psilocybin and psilocin. These alkaloidal chemicals are potent psychoactive substances which are illegal to possess. The top photograph shows a large bract fungus on a branch of *koa* (*Acacia koa*). The bottom photograph shows one inch tall fruiting bodies of a mushroom species.

Lichens (*Limu*)

As noted earlier, *limu* is a general Hawaiian name for many types of algae, liverworts, mosses, and lichens, e.g., *limu haea* is the name for *Sterocaulon vulcani* (shown below), which occurs on lava flows. Lichens appear to be individual plants; however, in reality they are unified combinations of algal and fungal components. The alga provides energy through photosynthesis, and the fungus provides moisture and mineral salts absorbed from the soil, plant, or rock medium on which the lichen grows. Water is absorbed in both liquid and vapor form. Lichens growing on rocks (*unahi pōhaku*) play an important role in the formation of soil by covering bare rock and helping initiate the decomposition processes.

The many forms of lichen are lumped into three general types: crustose (crustlike); foliose (leaflike), and fruticose (branching or cylindrical). Collectively, lichens comprise a very large group of plants, including more than 16,000 species. Lichens occur in a great variety of habitats, including many of the environments found in the ecologically diverse Hawaiian Islands. The tiny wind-blown reproductive bodies of lichens are among the first colonizers of new lava flows. Some lichens are found in dry areas; others occupy the wetter environments. Some lichens also occur above the tree line in the harsh alpine environments of Mauna Loa and Mauna Kea where they can survive the rigors of a severe climate.

Māmane, Māmani (E)
Sophora chrysophylla
Family: Fabaceae

Description

Māmame is an shrub or tree up to 45 ft. tall. A member of the pea or bean family, this woody species produces pinnately compound leaves, with many leaflets. Flowers are about an inch long and yellow. The mature brown pods are 1-6 inches long, four-winged, and constricted between the seeds.

Distribution

This endemic Hawaiian species is found scattered in a wide range of habitats, including dry shrubland and forest, as well as wetter areas from about 1,000 to over 9,000 feet elevation on all main islands except Niʻihau and Kahoʻolawe. It is still a dominant species in the subalpine vegetation of areas of East Maui and Hawaiʻi Island. In many places, extensive grazing and browsing by feral and domesticated hoofed mammals, particularly cattle, sheep, and goats, has greatly reduced the growth, and possible future existence of *māmane*.

Uses

Māmane produces hard, long-lasting wood which is used in fences. In ancient Hawaiʻi the wood was used to make house posts, sled runners, and digging sticks. The attractive yellow flowers of this plant were sometimes woven into garlands (*lei*). The photograph below shows a small *māmane* tree with other plants in a subalpine shrubland environment at about 7,500 ft. on the slopes of Mauna Loa, Hawaiʻi.

Naio, Naeo, Naieo (I)

Myoporum sandwicense
Family: Myoporaceae

Description

Naio is a variable, many-branched shrub or small tree up to about 45 ft. tall. Leaves, which differ in shape (2-8 inches long) have pointed tips and tend to be fleshy. The small flowers grow in axillary clusters, and are white, white with purplish specks, or occasionally pink. Fruits are small, greenish white to pinkish or purplish, and contain hard seeds.

Distribution

Because this species is also native to Mangaia, one of the Cook Islands, it is classified as an indigenous species in Hawai'i. It has a wide distribution in the Hawaiian Islands, from sea level to over 7,000 ft. It occurs in the coastal strand vegetation, on clinker (*'a'ā*) lava, in dry to wet forests, and in subalpine forests where it is often co-dominant with *māmane* (*Sophora chrysophlla*).

Uses

Naio wood was used to make house posts. It was also used to make mesh gauges utilized in the production of fishing nets. When it is dried or burned, the hard, dark yellow-green wood of *naio* has a scent like that of sandalwood (*'iliahi*). Cargo of *naio* wood sent to China in the 19th century as a substitute for native Hawaiian sandalwood was rejected (see *iliahi*, page 21). *Naio* is sometimes referred to as "bastard sandalwood."

Kūkaenēnē, 'Aiakanēnē, Leponēnē, Nēnē, Pūnēnē (E)
Coprosma ernodeoides
Family: Rubiaceae

Description
Similar to the other *Coprosma* species (see pages 54-55), this endemic, prostrate, multi-branched shrub is dioecious (i.e., male and female flowers are segregated on separate plants). *Coprosma ernodeoides*, which can root at its nodes, produces small, stiff, shiny, closely spaced, pointed leaves, 1/2 inch long or less. The small berry-like fruit are rounded, glossy, and black. Some of the Hawaiian names for this plant refer to its associations with the endemic, endangered *nēnē* goose, the official State bird of Hawai'i. *Kūkaenēnē*, for example, literally means "goose dung." And *'aiakanēnē* means "food of the *nēnē* goose."

Distribution
This low lying endemic shrub, with its attractive shiny dark fruit, is usually found in open places, frequently on lava and cinder deposits in wooded subalpine areas, 3,500-8,000 ft. on East Maui and Hawai'i Island. It also occurs occasionally in wet forest.

Uses
The inner bark of *kūkaenēnē* stems was used in ancient Hawai'i to make a yellow dye; and the fruit was used to make a purple to black dye. Fruits of this plant were also sometimes used in the fabrication of traditional garlands (*lei*).

'Āheahea, 'Āweoweo (E)

Chenopodium oahuense
Family: Chenopodiaceae

Description

'Āheahea (or *'āweoweo*) is an endemic, scentless or nearly scentless shrub (sometimes tree-like in form). The woody stems are erect (up to 7 ft. long) in higher elevations, or somewhat ascending to prostrate in lower elevation habitats, where the plant is only a few feet tall. The leaves are variable, normally 3-lobed, and usually have a dense cover of small, course, grayish hairs. One Hawaiian name for this plant, *'āheahea*, refers to the wilted appearance of the leaves. Flowers and fruits are numerous and small, produced in upright clusters at stem endings. The tiny seeds are dark brown. Other native names for this native shrub are *'ahea*, *'āhewahewa*, *alaweo*, *alaweo huna* (Ni'ihau), and *kāha'iha'i*.

Distribution

The genus *Chenopodium* contains more than 70 species. Some of these species (4-5) are now alien weeds in various areas of the Hawaiian Islands. At least 2 species of *Chenopodium* that grow wild in Hawai'i are known as *'āheahea*. One (*C. murale*) is an introduced weedy herb; the other (*C. oahuense*) is the endemic shrub shown here, which apparently has its closest relative in South America. Native *'āheahea* occurs as an occasional or common plant in dry habitats, coastal areas, dry forests, and subalpine shrubland, up to almost 8,000 ft. elevation, on all main Hawaiian Islands except Kaho'olawe, but most frequently on the high plains of Hawai'i Island. The more prostrate form of this species is also found on the low lying northwest Hawaiian Islands of Nihoa, Necker, French Frigate Shoals, Laysan, and Lisianski. The *'āheahea* shown here were photographed in the saddle region at about 6,000 ft. elevation between Mauna Kea and Mauna Loa on Hawai'i Island. The genus name *Chenopodium* refers to the general leaf shape of these plants which resembles a "goose-foot."

Uses

In times of food scarcity, young, tender leaves of *'āheahea* were wrapped in the leaves of *ti* (*Cordyline fruticosa*) and cooked on heated coals. The wood of the native *'āheahea* was sometimes used in the construction of composite fishhooks, such as those used to make *makau manō* (shark hooks).

Nohoanu, Hinahina (E)
Geranium spp.
Family: Geraniaceae

Description
There are approximately 300 species in the genus *Geranium*. A number of these plants are cultivated for their attractive flowers or scented leaves. There are 6 endemic species of *Geranium* in Hawai‘i. There are also 5 alien species in this genus which are now naturalized in Hawai‘i. Although the great majority of *Geranium* species are herbs, the native Hawaiian members of this genus are shrubs or subshrubs. They produce leaves with margins that are smooth, except at the tips, which are toothed or serrated. The flowers of the native Hawaiian species have 5 white, pink, purple, or reddish petals.

Distribution
Two Hawaiian names for the endemic *Geranium* species of these islands are *nohoanu*, which refers to plants that dwell

in cold places, and *hinahina*, which refers to the grayish leaf hair color of some plants. The native *Geranium* species are found in the higher, cooler, upland regions on Hawai‘i, Maui, and Kaua‘i Islands. Grayish leaf hairs help reflect some wave lengths of solar radiation, thus protecting the plants from excessive ultraviolet exposure and desiccation in high montane or subalpine environments. The species shown in a subalpine area of Mauna Kea (top right photo) is *Geranium cuneatum*, a native, compact, erect, many-branched shrub up to 3 ft. tall with many grayish hairs on the leaves. It occurs on Hawai‘i and Haleakalā, Maui in subalpine shrubland and forest, alpine shrubland, and as an early colonizer of shrubland on lava where fog is common. The species shown on the bottom left is *Geranium multiflorum*. It is found in montane grassland or moist forest, and sometimes in subalpine shrubland, from 4,500 to 7,500 ft. on East Maui. The other 4 endemic species are found in subalpine shrubland (*G. arboreum*) or in bogs (*G. hanaense*, *G. humile*, and *G. kauaiense*).

Silversword Alliance (E)

Argyroxiphium, Dubautia, Wilkesia
Family: Asteraceae

Description and Distribution

The silversword alliance includes 28 endemic species (belonging to the sunflower
family) in 3 endemic genera (*Argyroxiphium*,
5 spp., *Dubautia*, 21 spp., and *Wilkesia*, 2
spp.). Numerous natural and artificial cross-
ing between species in different genera of the
silversword alliance have produced hybrids,
indicating close relationships. All species in
the alliance are believed to have evolved in
Hawai'i from a single, ancestral North American tarweed species. The silversword alliance
is an outstanding example of adaptive radiation. *Argyroxiphium* spp.(shrubs) are all endangered with extinction, including the fa-
mous, so-called Haleakalā silversword, known
in Hawaiian as *'āhinahina* or *hinahina*
(*Argyroxiphium sandwicense*, top right). It is
found in alpine cinder cone deserts on East Maui and Mauna Kea. *'Āhinahina* is well
adapted to these high mountain areas. Its rosette of long, fleshy, low lying leaves protects
the plant from chilling winds; and the silvery leaf hairs reduce damage from harsh sun-
light and collect fog drip in these arid areas. After 7-20 years of vegetative growth, the
plant produces a tall stalk of many flower heads. Then, following seed development and
dispersal, the plant dies. There are two other silversword species, the Ka'ū silversword (*A.
kauense*), found in a few forest and bog areas on Hawai'i Island, and the 'Eke silversword
(*A. caliginis*), found in summit bogs of West Maui. Two "greenswords" (*A. grayanum* and
A. virescens), which lack the silvery leaf color, occur in upper wet forests of Maui. *Dubautia*
contains 21 species of shrubs, trees, and lianas, many known as *na'ena'e* or *kupaoa*. Shown
below are *D. ciliolata* (bottom left, common in open, dry places between 2,000-9,500 ft. on
Hawai'i Island) and *D. menziesii* (found in the subalpine and alpine areas of East Maui,
including Haleakalā "crater"). Both species of *Wilkesia* are rare erect shrubs found only on
Kaua'i (*W. gymnoxiphium*, known as *iliau*, is shown in Waimea Canyon, see back cover).

ʻŌhiʻa lehua (*Metrosideros*) with Mauna Kea volcano in the distance.

A Short Bibliography for Further Study

Abbott, Isabella A. 1992. *Lāʻau Hawaiʻi: Traditional Hawaiian Uses of Plants*. Bishop Museum Press, Honolulu, Hawaiʻi. 163 pp.

Carlquist, Sherwin. 1980. *Hawaii: A Natural History*. Pacific Tropical Botanical Garden, Lawai, Kauaʻi. 2nd Edition. 468 pp.

Degener, Otto. 1930. *Plants of Hawaii National Park*. Photolithoprint edition (1945). Edward Brothers, Ann Arbor. 314 pp.

Krauss, Beatrice H. 1993. *Plants in Hawaiian Culture*. University of Hawaii Press. Honolulu, Hawaii. 345 pp.

Lamoureux, Charles. 1976. *Trailside Plants of Hawaii's National Parks*. Hawaiʻi Natural History Association, Hawaiʻi. 79 pp.

Merlin, Mark. 1986. *Hawaiian Coastal Plants*. Oriental Publishing Co. Honolulu, Hawaiʻi. 68 pp.

Neal, Marie C. 1965. *In Gardens of Hawaii*. Bishop Museum Press, Honolulu, Hawaiʻi. 924 pp.

Sohmer, S.H. and Robert Gustafson. 1987. *Plants and Flowers of Hawaiʻi*.University of Hawaii Press, Honolulu, Hawaiʻi. 160 pp.

Wagner, Warren L., Herbst, Derral R. and S.H. Sohmer. 1990. *Manual of the Flowering Plants of Hawaiʻi*. Bishop Museum Spec. Pub. 83. UH Press and Bishop Museum Press, Honolulu, Hawaii. 2 Vols., 1,853 pp.

Whistler, W. Arthur. 1992. *Flowers of the Pacific Island Seashore*. Isle Botanica, Honolulu, Hawaiʻi. 154 pp.

Published by Pacific Guide Books
1261 Center St., Honolulu, Hawaiʻi 96816
Printed by China Color Printing Co., Inc.
Taipei, Taiwan, Rep. of China
Revised 4th Edition 1995